JOSE MARTI

Cuban Patriot and Poet

David Goodnough

Enslow Publishers, Inc.

40 Industrial Road   PO Box 38
Box 398   Aldershot
Berkeley Heights, NJ 07922   Hants GU12 6BP
USA   UK

http://www.enslow.com

Library of Congress Cataloging-in-Publication Data

Goodnough, David.
    José Martí : Cuban patriot and poet / David Goodnough.
       p. cm. — (Hispanic biographies)
    Includes bibliographical references (p.   ) and index.
    Summary: A biography of the famous writer and poet who inspired Cubans to
fight for their freedom from the Spanish.
    ISBN 0-89490-761-1
    1. Martí, José, 1853–1895— Juvenile literature. 2. Cuba—History—
1810–1899—Juvenile literature. 3. Statesmen—Cuba—Biography—Juvenile
literature. 4. Revolutionaries—Cuba—Biography—Juvenile literature. 5. Authors,
Cuban—19th century—Biography—Juvenile literature. [1. Martí, José, 1853–
1895. 2. Cuba—History—1810–1899. 3. Revolutionaries. 4. Authors, Cuban.]
I. Title. II. Series.
F1983.M37G66   1996
972.08'1'092—dc20
  [B]   95-33246
                                        CIP
                                        AC
Printed in the United States of America

10 9 8 7 6 5 4 3

Our America Copyright © 1975 by Philip S. Foner. Reprinted by permission of
Monthly Review Foundation; *Inside the Monster* Copyright © 1975 by Philip S.
Foner. Reprinted by permission of Monthly Review Foundation; *On Art & Literature*
Copyright © 1982 by Philip S. Foner. Reprinted by permission of Monthly Review
Foundation.

Illustration Credits: Organization of American States, pp. 7, 9, 25, 29, 76,
97; Author's collection, pp. 16, 18, 20, 33, 42, 50, 59, 65, 70, 90, 113;
New York Public Library Picture Collection, pp. 53, 83, 104; Warner
Brothers, p. 115.

Cover Illustration: Organization of American States

CONTENTS

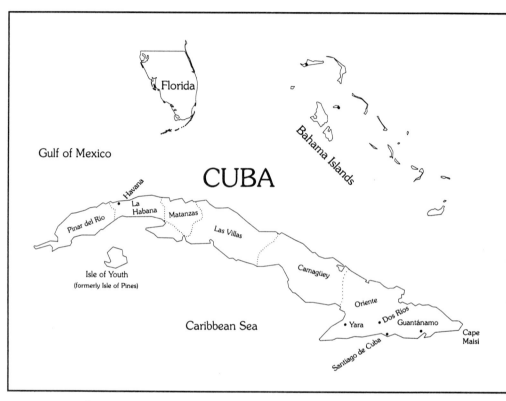

Florida

Gulf of Mexico

Bahama Islands

CUBA

Havana
La
Habana

Pinar del Río

Matanzas

Las Villas

Isle of Youth
(formerly Isle of Pines)

Camagüey

Oriente

Yara • • Dos Ríos
Guantánamo

Caribbean Sea

Santiago de Cuba

Cape
Maisi

José Martí was born in Havana, Cuba on January 28, 1853.

CHAPTER ONE

His Hour
Had Come

José Martí sat on a hilltop near Dos Ríos, Cuba, writing a letter to a friend. Martí was a famous poet and writer who, in his lifetime, had written thousands of letters. This was to be his last, and it was never finished.

The letter was dated May 18, 1895. A little more than one month before, Martí and four other men had landed on the eastern coast of Cuba. Their purpose was to begin a war of independence to free Cuba from Spain. They had marched 140 miles westward from their landing place, joining with other groups of men along the way. By the time they reached Dos Ríos, they had a small army of more than four hundred men and three hundred horses.[1] They had fought many small battles along the way, and had won most of them. However, they had not yet met a large enemy army.

Martí wrote in his letter: "I am in daily danger of giving my life for my country and duty, for I understand that duty and have the courage to carry it out."[2] Martí, a thin, frail man who walked with a slight limp, had spent most of his life studying, writing, teaching, and making speeches. But now he was a general in the army that he had inspired to rise up against the Spanish government.

His duty, as he saw it, was to gain Cuba's independence from Spain and to prevent any other country from taking it over. He wrote: "All I have done so far, and all I will do, is for this purpose."[3] He never finished his letter because word came that there were many Spanish soldiers nearby and a battle would soon take place.

The next day—May 19, 1895—the commanding general of the rebel army, Máximo Gómez, decided to attack the Spanish. This could be their largest battle yet, so he ordered Martí to stay behind in the camp with a small group of soldiers. Many believed that if the revolution were successful, Martí would be the new president of

José Martí, 1853-1895.

the Republic of Cuba. Therefore, he was much too valuable to risk his life in battle. Besides, even though Martí had been made a major general by Gómez, he had no military training or experience.

Martí, however, was anxious to see action. He also wanted to prove to the Cuban people that he was not a man "who preached the need of dying and then did not begin by risking his life. Wherever my first duty may lie . . . there I will be. . . . But my one desire would be to stay there close beside the last tree, the last fighter, and die quietly. For my hour has come."[4]

Soon after the main army left the camp, Martí heard heavy firing. Gómez and his men had run into heavy enemy resistance. Martí leaped onto a white horse and rode toward the sound of the gunfire. In the confusion of battle, both the rebels and the Spanish were surprised to see Martí ride headlong into the midst of the fighting. A Spanish soldier recognized Martí and shouted for his comrades to fire on him. A bullet struck Martí in the chest, and he fell from the saddle. He died almost immediately.

The rebels tried to recover Martí's body, but were unable to fight through the enemy lines. The Spanish buried the body nearby, but when they learned that it was the famous José Martí, they

A monument was built at the site where José Martí was killed in battle, at Dos Ríos, Cuba.

dug it up and took it to nearby Santiago de Cuba. There they buried him with respect.

In the years to come, a shrine would be erected over Martí's grave, and statues of him and monuments to him would be erected throughout Cuba, including a huge structure in the central square of Havana. His carved likeness can be found in every public school, and all cities and towns of any size in Cuba have at least one street named after him.

Today, many historians and political writers have concluded that José Martí did more for the liberation of Cuba than any other Cuban who ever lived.

WHERE THE PALM
TREE GROWS

"Yo soy un hombre sincero, de donde crece la palma" ("I am an honest man, from where the palm tree grows"), wrote José Martí in one of his most famous poems.[1] That is exactly what early Cuba was to most of the world—the land "where the palm tree grows"—and not much more. The first Europeans to visit Cuba were sailors from Columbus's first voyage in 1492. Columbus landed there only briefly, in order to claim it for Spain, and then moved east to a nearby island that he named Hispaniola. Since Cuba did not have much of the gold and silver that

the Spanish were searching for, it was not considered as important as the other lands around the Caribbean Sea. It was made a colony in 1511, but was used mostly as a stopover for the Spanish ships that were carrying soldiers and missionaries to the rich lands farther to the west. Havana thus became an important seaport.

A few settlers stayed on the island and established small farms or plantations on which they raised cattle and a little coffee, tobacco, and sugar. For workers, they used the Arawak and Ciboney natives of the island and the few slaves that the Spanish government allowed them to bring over from Africa. The native people suffered greatly from the hard working conditions and cruel treatment imposed by their Spanish masters. They also caught many diseases from the Spanish, notably smallpox. The native people, who had lived apart from the rest of the world, had built up no resistance to these diseases, and they soon began to die off. Since Cuba contributed little in the way of wealth to the Spanish Empire, the government in Spain paid little attention to it and its problems.

Havana, now the capital city of Cuba, was occupied by the British for a brief time (1762 to 1763) during Europe's Seven Years War; and for the first time, Cuban landowners were able to sell some of their products to the rest of the world, not just to Spain. Ironically, the greatest improvement in Cuba's economy came in the 1790s as a result of a slave rebellion on the nearby island of Hispaniola, which today is divided into the independent republic of Haiti and the Dominican Republic. France controlled Haiti for several years, mainly as a result of Spain's lack of interest in the western part of the island. For years, English and French pirates had used it as a base for their raids on Spanish ships. Eventually, some of the French settled on the coast and began working farms and sugar plantations. Within a few years, Haiti had become the world's leading sugar producer. In order to work this large crop, the French imported great numbers of African slaves, who soon began to outnumber their French owners.

During the French Revolution of 1789, the French government lost control of its overseas empire, and the slaves of Haiti took this chance to overthrow their masters. After a bloody war, they took complete control of the colony. The French planters and plantation owners fled to Cuba, where they started up their sugar plantations again. Soon the production and shipping of sugar became Cuba's major industry and source of wealth, and it was based almost wholly on slave labor.

Spain now began to take an interest in the colony. It sent over more government officials and increased taxes on all of Cuba's exports and imports, along with heavy taxes on land. The wealthy landowners of Cuba were mostly Spaniards who had been born in Cuba. They were known as *Criollos.* Those who were born in Spain and who usually represented the Spanish government in Cuba were known as *peninsulares* because they came from the Spanish peninsula across the sea.

The Cuban Criollos resented Spain's control over their trade with other nations and its heavy taxation of them. They were also angry because they had no control over their government but were completely at the mercy of the peninsulares. The Cuban Criollos, however, did not go so far as to call for a complete break from Spain. By this time, the population of Cuba was almost one-quarter African-Cuban, due to the increasing number of slaves used to work on the sugar plantations. The Cuban Criollos had learned from the violent revolution in Haiti that any troubles between them and the mother country might give the slaves the opportunity to revolt, so they did their best to get along with Spain, asking only that they be given a say in their own government.

By the 1820s, Cuba and Puerto Rico were the last remaining Spanish colonies in the Western

Hemisphere, and Spain guarded them closely. Any attempt by the Cuban Criollos to change either the government or the way of doing business was discouraged and opposed by Spain. A small group of Cuban Criollos was so dissatisfied with Spain's treatment of them that they began to talk about becoming part of the United States, their close neighbor to the north.

At that time, the world was moving toward a complete ban on slavery; the United States and Cuba were almost alone in continuing to use slave labor. The United States was also Cuba's greatest customer, so the two countries had a dual bond. At this time also, the United States was acquiring Texas and other lands from Mexico, so it seemed logical to make Cuba part of its lands around almost the whole of the Gulf of Mexico. The American Civil War and the consequent end of slavery in the United States, however, put an end to this talk.

The Cuban Criollos wanted more control of their government, and they wanted to keep their slaves, but they realized that Spain would never allow it. The only solution to their problem seemed to be to win their independence from Spain, by war if necessary.

In October of 1868, a Cuban Criollo landowner named Carlos de Céspedes issued the

Carlos Manuel de Céspedes issued the "Cry from Yara," which started the Ten Years War on October 10, 1868.

"Grito de Yara" ("Cry from Yara"). This declaration of Cuba's independence and call to action was issued from the town of Yara in southeastern Cuba. Céspedes called upon all Cubans to take up arms and expel the corrupt and greedy colonial government.

The war that followed lasted for ten years (1868–1878) and was waged mostly in the rough eastern part of the island, Oriente province. The army of the Cuban rebels consisted primarily of poorly armed and organized Criollo farmers and freed slaves. They quarreled among themselves, sometimes refused to fight away from their homes, and were never able to win a battle important enough to rally the rest of the Cuban people behind them. They were also unable to win the support of the western part of the island, Occidente province, where the wealthy Cuban Criollo landowners continued to support Spain.

However, two heroes arose from this conflict. The first was not a Cuban, but a native of the Dominican Republic, which shared the island of Hispaniola with Haiti. He was Máximo Gómez, the leader of the Cuban Liberating Army, which was one of the few traditional military organizations on the rebel side. The other, Antonio Maceo, was an expert in the type of guerrilla warfare waged by Cubans in the

General Máximo Gómez, a citizen of the Dominican Republic, was a hero of the Ten Years War.

mountains and plains of Oriente province. Although the war was finally lost, these two men remained an inspiration to Cubans in the years to come. The war also inspired a sense of patriotism in ordinary Cubans, who felt pride in their stubborn battle against the better equipped and much larger Spanish army.

The war, which became known in Cuba as the Ten Years War, ended with the Treaty of Zanjón in 1878. The Spanish government promised various reforms, including the granting of government representation to native Cubans, but their promises were not kept. What followed was another period of discontent. The war had had a terrible effect on Cuba's economy, and many sugar plantations had been ruined. Some rebels who had never surrendered continued fighting in the mountains over the next seventeen years. General Gómez retired to his home in Santo Domingo in the Dominican Republic but continued to keep in touch with Cuban affairs.

Antonio Maceo refused to surrender and denounced the Treaty of Zanjón in ringing words that made him famous at home and abroad. In exile in Mexico, he continued to urge Cubans to resist the Spanish and to work toward the goal of independence. Maceo was part African-Cuban, and he was particularly interested in ending slavery

General Antonio Maceo was another Cuban hero of the
Ten Years War.

in Cuba. He became a national hero in Cuba and kept alive the pride of ordinary Cubans in themselves and their country. The poor farmers and slaves, both freed and unfree, were strong supporters of Maceo.

Due to increasing pressure from the nations of Europe, especially England, Spain formally abolished slavery in 1886. Now the Cuban Criollos no longer had the protection of the government in their relations with their slaves, so the last reason for a tie with Spain was broken. Complete independence now seemed more and more attractive to all native Cubans.

TREASON!

José Julián Martí y Pérez was born in Havana on January 28, 1853. His father, Mariano Martí, had come to Cuba as a sergeant in the Spanish army. His mother, Leonor Pérez Martí, had also been born in Spain, so both his parents were peninsulares. His father, who remained loyal to Spain throughout his life, served the government in a variety of military and government positions. A friend later wrote that José's parents "were honest, although possessing little intelligence or education."[1] Martí had seven sisters, but two of them died when very young.

José's father was a stern, no-nonsense civil servant who earned his living from the Spanish government. After his service in the army, he worked as a police officer and, later, as a night watchman in Havana and other cities. When José was four or five years old, his father took the whole family back to Spain, where he hoped to recover from an illness. After two years in Spain, the family returned to Cuba, and José's father again found a job as a guard. Therefore, at a very young age, José became accustomed to frequent travel and changes of address.

In 1862, Martí's father was made a minor government official in Hanábana, a district in western Cuba. He took his young son with him and made him a clerk in his office. José proved to be excellent at this type of work, and his father hoped that he would follow it as a career. But it was while he was in Hanábana that José witnessed firsthand the cruelty of landowners and overseers to the African slaves who worked on the plantations. In a poem written much later, Martí described a scene in which slaves mourn for a man who has been hanged from a tree:

> *Un niño lo vio: tembló*
> *De pasión por los que gimen:*
> *¡Y, al pie del muerto, juró*
> *Lavar con su vida el crimen!*[2]

(A small boy saw it. He trembled
With feeling for the groaning men,
And at the victim's feet he vowed
To cleanse the crime with his life.)

José's mother, who was much gentler and
more understanding than his father, wanted the
boy to continue his education. His father thought
that further schooling was a waste of time and too
expensive. His mother got her way, however,
when José's godfather agreed to pay for his
further education.

Martí was enrolled in the Municipal School for
Boys in Havana.

At school, José was noticed by Rafael María de
Mendive, a famous teacher, poet, editor, and
patriot who believed strongly in the need for
Cuban independence. Mendive took an interest in
the boy and paid special attention to him. While
he taught José to appreciate poetry and literature,
he also urged him to become aware of the political
and social situation in Cuba. José became almost a
member of Mendive's family and spent long hours
listening to the literary and political talk among the
visitors to the house.

Mendive was also director of St. Paul's School,
a branch of the Municipal School for Boys. José
attended this school and became one of its star
pupils. Mendive encouraged him to write in his

José Martí was born on January 28, 1853, in this house in Havana, Cuba.

free time and to engage in the literary activities of the school.

José was fifteen years old when the Ten Years War broke out. He was firmly on the side of the rebels because of Mendive's influence and also because of his own feelings about Spanish colonialism. He was too young to join any of the rebel forces, so he decided to lend his literary skills to the cause.

José and a friend named Fermín Valdés Domínguez, with the help of Mendive, produced a pamphlet called *El diablo cojuelo* (The Limping Devil). In it, they poked fun at the Spanish captain general of Havana. The general could not have been amused because he had, after all, lifted the ban on the freedom of the press that had been in place since the beginning of the war. A few days later, José published a small newspaper on his own, again aided by Mendive, called *La Patria Libre* (The Free Country). This paper also did not go over well with the authorities. It contained Martí's first drama, a short play called *Abdala,* in which the main character sounds very much like José himself. At one point in the play, Abdala says, "I will be the one to free my anguished country, and the one who will drag the oppressor from the people."[3] A few days after the appearance of the newspaper, Mendive was falsely accused of having been behind a political demonstration against the government. He was found guilty and sent into exile. This was the way the colonial government got rid of people they considered troublemakers.

On October 4, 1869, José and a few of his friends gathered at the home of Fermín Valdés Domínguez. Most of the boys attended St. Paul's, and they liked to meet and talk about their lessons and their teachers and trade stories about their classmates. The weather was hot and sticky, and the windows of Fermín's house were open to the street to catch any breezes coming in from the harbor. The boys' voices and laughter could be heard throughout the neighborhood.

A group of Spanish *voluntarios* happened to pass by the house. The voluntarios were not regular soldiers but a sort of militia that served the Spanish army in Cuba. They patrolled the inner city and watched out for any civilian troublemakers. The boys spotted the group and began to make jokes about their appearance. They were only making fun of the way the voluntarios tried to act like regular soldiers, but some of the voluntarios did not take the teasing well. Many scowls and threatening looks were directed at the house. Eventually, the voluntarios went on their way, and the boys returned to their talk.

José and Fermín had learned recently that a former student of Mendive's had joined the Spanish voluntarios. The two boys had written an angry letter to the student, criticizing him for his action, which went against everything their master had taught them. After they cooled down, the boys had decided not to send or publish the letter, but neither had thought to destroy it.

Now there was suddenly a loud banging on the door and shouted demands to open up. It was the voluntarios, who had returned from their patrol. They brushed past the boys and began searching every corner of the house. It was not long before one of them reappeared, waving the letter José and Fermín had written.

All of the boys present were taken into custody, and José and Fermín were arrested and jailed. The charge? Disloyalty—or treason!

It was four and a half months before the boys were brought to trial. In the meantime, they were locked up in an overcrowded jail with hardened criminals. In early March of 1870, they were finally brought before a military court.

Both boys were already assumed guilty, but each attempted to take all the blame for writing the letter. The court asked each boy to state his case. José was by far the better speaker, and he argued his position so strongly that the court was

José Martí was kept in this building on the Isle of Pines in custody for one year before his exile to Spain. Almost every building or place connected with Martí is now a national shrine.

convinced that he was the more dangerous of the two. Fermín was sentenced to six months in prison; José was sentenced to six years!

José was not much over seventeen years of age when he was sent to do hard labor in Havana's stone quarry. He was put in chains and forced to break rocks under the boiling sun. At one point, he was struck with a chain by a guard. The resulting injury caused him to walk with a limp for the rest of his life. Fortunately, José's father had friends and connections in the army and in the stone quarry itself. Through their influence, José was released from the stone quarry after six months. His health was ruined, but his spirit survived. He was now more convinced than ever of the injustice of the Spanish colonial system and the need for Cuban independence.

José was put in the custody of the warden of the stone quarry, who had an estate on the Isle of Pines. On this island off the southern coast of Cuba, José recovered from his ordeal. In December of 1870, he returned to Havana. The court told José that they had decided to be lenient with him, but he was to be deported to Spain. The authorities had decided to get rid of another troublemaker, just as they had with Mendive.

On January 15, 1871, José left for Spain. He was to spend most of the rest of his life in exile.

Exile

In Spain, Martí was free to do as he pleased. He was, after all, a Spanish citizen. He found a job as a tutor to a wealthy family and enrolled in the Central University in Madrid. He studied law but also read the classics and attended the theater, concert halls, and art galleries. There were other Cuban exiles in Spain, and Martí soon became acquainted with them. One of the first things he did was turn to writing for the cause of Cuban independence. He wrote a pamphlet called *El presidio político en Cuba* (The Political Prison in Cuba), in which he tried to inform the Spanish public of the injustices of their colonial governors. He became well-known in literary and political circles and was frequently asked to write about Cuba for Spanish newspapers. He was also invited to speak at university gatherings. His subject was always the unjust situation in Cuba and the need for change.

Valdés Domínguez soon joined Martí in exile, and they took up where they had left off in Havana. Together, they produced a pamphlet entitled *The 27th of November!* It contained a poem by Martí dedicated to eight medical students who were shot by Spanish police for demonstrating in Havana on that date in 1871. The pamphlet called upon Cubans everywhere to swear "an oath of infinite love of country . . . over their bodies."[1] The pamphlet attracted much attention and, for the first time, brought the plight of Cuba to the attention of many of the Spanish people.

Spain was then still a monarchy, ruled by King Amadeus, and governed by a *Cortes*, or legislature. Martí believed that if Spain became a republic, its people would no longer stand for its colonial policy and would withdraw its army from Cuba. In February of 1873, a Spanish army corps mutinied and the king was forced to abdicate, or give up his throne. The first Spanish republic was established on February 11, 1873. Martí was in the press box

José Martí (seated) and his friend Fermín Valdés Domínguez were both convicted of treason and imprisoned by the Spanish government. Together, in exile, they wrote *The 27th of November!*

when the Cortes established the new government. He was delighted with the new order and the prospects for Cuba. However, when he heard one of the members of the new Cortes not only approve but praise Spain's colonial policy, he realized that nothing had changed.

Martí responded the way he usually did, by writing a pamphlet, *La República Española y la Revolución Cubana* (The Spanish Republic and the Cuban Revolution). In it, he argued that Cuba had the same right to govern itself as Spain did and that one republic should recognize the rights of another. His argument did not persuade the Cortes. Instead, it brought Martí to the attention of the authorities as a possible troublemaker.

Martí's health was still poor. This and his disappointment with the new Spanish republic led him to move to Zaragoza in northern Spain. Zaragoza was located in the province of Aragón, which had a long tradition of opposing the central government in Madrid, so Martí felt safer and more comfortable there, among people who felt the same as he did about the new Spanish republic. He had his credits transferred to the University of Zaragoza, where he continued to study law. He received his degree in law in June of 1874 and went on to obtain a degree in the liberal arts. He continued to work as a tutor, earning just enough to cover his living expenses.

The new Spanish republic fell in January of 1874, following more military revolts. Martí had by now withdrawn from any active role in Spanish politics, although he still kept himself informed of events. He was now free to travel outside of Spain, but as a political exile he could not return to Cuba, especially since the war for independence was still being fought there.

Martí was now twenty-two years old, and he had not seen his family for over four years. After Martí's exile, his family had moved to Mexico, and Martí decided to join them there. He and his old friend Valdés Domínguez left Spain for Paris, where they lingered for a few weeks to take in the atmosphere of what was then considered the capital of the world. From there they went to England and set sail from Southampton for Mexico. They arrived in Veracruz on February 8, 1875. Martí was reunited with his family, although the occasion was a sad one because his favorite sister, Ana, had died while he was away. He was greeted happily by his father, who was now proud of his educated son's accomplishments. Father and son had never been close, and Mariano Martí had been angered by his son's conviction for treason. Now, however, he had softened his opinion of Martí's political activities. He never stood in his son's way again.

Martí's first task in his new land was to find employment, and that meant, of course, a writing job. Through the influence of a family friend, Manuel Mercado, Martí was hired by Mexico City's *La Revista Universal* (The Universal Review). This was a weekly newspaper that covered literary and artistic affairs as well as national news. Martí soon became one of the most important members of the newspaper's staff. He published poems as well as articles on Mexico City's cultural life, using the pen name "Orestes." He also issued bulletins detailing Mexico's progress under its liberal government. Under his own name, he wrote articles on Spanish and Cuban politics. He paid particular attention to the Mexican Indian's place in Mexican life. This interest in minorities and their place in the government began when he was in Mexico and was to last for his lifetime. As he wrote in one of his poems:

> *Con los pobres de la tierra*
> *Quiero yo mi suerte echar:*
> *El arroyo de la sierra*
> *Me complace más que el mar.*[2]

(With the poor of this world
I want to cast my lot.
A mountain stream to me
Means more than the sea.)

Martí had made himself a respected public figure in Mexico. His views on everything from the theater to the political situation in Central America were eagerly awaited. In January of 1876, he was asked by workers in Chihuahua to be their spokesperson at a national labor congress. This was something new for Martí. Until now he had mingled mostly in literary and political circles. During this time, he also managed to publish a translation into Spanish of Victor Hugo's novel *Mes Fils* (My Sons), and to write a short play. This play, entitled *Amor con amor se paga* (Love Is Repaid With Love), was presented successfully by a Mexico City theatrical company. Also during this time, he met Carmen Zayas Bazán, the daughter of a wealthy Cuban aristocrat in exile in Mexico.

In the late fall of 1876, the political situation in Mexico had reached a state of crisis. General Porfirio Díaz had staged a military coup and forced President Lerdo de Tejada to flee the capital. Martí had admired and supported the president, and he was disappointed to see him overthrown by Díaz, a man whom everyone had thought was a liberal who believed in democracy. This planted in Martí the seed of distrust and suspicion of all military men who gave their promise to support popular government.

Martí decided to leave Mexico. Even though he was now an important member of the Mexican community, he had continued to work for the cause of Cuban independence. He had learned that the war for independence was not going well for the rebels. Part of this was due to differences in purpose within rebel ranks. General Antonio Maceo wanted most of all to free the slaves. His fellow generals felt that if they did, they would lose the support of the Cuban Criollo landowners. Therefore, the movement for independence had the full support of neither the African Cubans nor the Cuban Criollo landowners and farmers. Martí felt that he might be able to do something to solve this problem simply by being there. He was well-known and admired in Cuba because he was both the rebels' spokesman to the rest of the world and their chief supporter and fundraiser.

On January 6, 1877, Martí arrived in Cuba, traveling under the name Julián Pérez, which was a combination of his middle name and his mother's family name. Martí soon learned that the rebels' situation was desperate. They had suffered heavy losses with no apparent gains, and the countryside was suffering from the desolation brought about by the war. The heavy taxation Spain demanded in order to pay for the war had ruined whole businesses. The destruction of sugar mills and plantations that had been caught in the path of the war had caused widespread unemployment. The United States had decided to side with Spain, thus denying the rebels badly needed supplies. In short, the situation was hopeless. Seeing that he could do nothing, Martí sadly returned to Mexico.

Martí did not wish to stay in Mexico under the dictatorship of General Díaz. His old friend Valdés Domínguez recommended that he try Guatemala, even lending him the money to get there. Martí arrived in Guatemala City in March of 1877 and immediately sought out any Cubans who might be living there. He soon met José María Izaguirre, another exiled Cuban, who was director of Guatemala's Central School. Izaguirre believed as strongly as Martí in the need for an independent Cuba, so the two men took to each other immediately. Izaguirre had heard of Martí and had read some of his political articles. He was most impressed, however, with Martí's educational background and achievements. Because Martí spoke French and English and was well grounded in Latin and Greek, Izaguirre had no trouble getting him appointed to the faculty of the Central School. So Martí embarked on another profession, this time as a teacher of history and literature.

During all of this time, Martí had been engaged to marry Carmen Zayas Bazán, who was still living in Mexico with her family. In Guatemala, Martí met and became friends with General Miguel García Granado. The general had a daughter named María, and Martí fell in love with her. His engagement to Carmen, however, prevented him from asking María to marry him. Martí's dilemma was solved in a most unfortunate way: María died, most likely from tuberculosis. In her memory, Martí wrote one of his finest poems, *La niña de Guatemala* (The Young Woman of Guatemala). He says of her:

> *Ella, por volverlo a ver,*
> *Salió a verlo al mirador;*
> *Él volvió con su mujer;*
> *Ella se murió de amor . . .*
> *Dicen que murió de frío:*
> *Yo sé que murió de amor.*[3]

> (Wanting to see his return,
> She went up to the belvedere.
> He had returned with a wife.
> She died of love. . . .
> They say she died of cold;
> I know she died of love.)

In December of 1877, Martí returned to Mexico and married Carmen. He then returned to Guatemala with his young wife and plunged into the literary life of the capital. He edited the university's newspaper, he lectured, and he began writing a history of Guatemala. He founded and took part in several literary and artistic clubs and became one of the best-known figures in Guatemala City's social and political life.

The president of Guatemala at this time was Justo Rufino Barrios, a liberal politician who had set out to modernize his country and bring relief to the poor and peasant classes. Martí was impressed by Barrios, particularly by his attempts to curb the power of the Catholic church. However, Barrios ruled with an iron hand, and he had little use for democracy or the opinions of the people. Martí was shocked when Barrios had eight priests executed merely for demonstrating against him.

A rumor spread through Guatemala's Central School that Izaguirre was neglecting his duties. President Barrios called Izaguirre before him to explain his conduct. Izaguirre felt insulted that his performance as director of the school should even be questioned, and he resigned in protest. Martí also resigned in loyalty to Izaguirre.

Martí could now devote himself full-time to writing, but he had difficulty earning enough money to support himself and his young wife, who was expecting a child. Then, in September 1878, the war in Cuba came to an end. One of the terms

Carmen Zayas Bazán, the daughter of a Cuban exile in Mexico, married José Martí on December 20, 1877.

of the peace agreement between the rebels and the government was that all Cubans convicted of political crimes be granted a complete pardon. Martí's name was high on the list of those whose sentences were set aside, and he was now free to return to Cuba legally.

A LITTLE WAR

 The Treaty of Zanjón, which ended the Ten Years War, gave Cubans a small measure of self-government, but the Spanish government soon ignored or bypassed the treaty. Wealthy Cuban landowners continued to support Spain as their only means of keeping their slaves, who together with the poorer farmers greatly outnumbered them. In short, nothing changed.

On November 22, 1878, Martí's son, José, was born, and Martí now had family responsibilities. He tried to practice law, but he was denied a license because of his past prison record. He found work as an assistant in the office of a distinguished Cuban lawyer, Nicolás Azacarte, who had also been an exile in Mexico. Also working in Azacarte's office was Juan Gualberto Gómez, a revolutionary writer who had not given up on the cause of true Cuban independence. Soon he and Martí were turning out pamphlets that promoted the cause of a free Cuba.

The revolutionary spirit was still alive in Cuba, and veterans of the war who had fled abroad formed a Cuban Revolutionary Committee. The headquarters of this organization was in New York City, and from there the committee issued a call for all Cubans to work for the cause of independence. Many Cubans answered this call by setting up underground organizations in Cuba to assist in any future uprising.

Martí was beginning to regret that he had ever returned to Cuba. He wrote:

> I was not born to live in these lands. Exile in one's country is a thousand times more bitter for those, like myself, who have found a home in exile. Here I do not speak, nor write, nor do I have the energy to think.[1]

In his speeches, he began to refer to Cuba as "our nation."[2] and became ever more insistent that the only solution to the country's problems was complete freedom from Spain. He became more and more aggressive, once stating that rights were "to be taken, not requested; seized, not begged for."[3] Havana's Captain General Ramón Blanco was in the audience when Martí made that statement, and he said later, "That Martí is a madman—but a dangerous madman."[4]

On August 26, 1879, revolutionary feelings reached their peak when hundreds of farmers and slaves attacked the Spanish stronghold in Santiago de Cuba. Riots and demonstrations against the government broke out all over Cuba. *La Guerra Chiquita* (The Little War) as it was called, was soon almost crushed. The government moved to prevent any further uprisings by imprisoning all known troublemakers and clamping down on all publications and public meetings. Martí's friend and fellow revolutionary Juan Gualberto Gómez was imprisoned, and Martí seemed fated to be next. Some politically powerful people came to his support, however, and the captain general agreed to a compromise. Martí could escape imprisonment if he would renounce his revolutionary views and support the Spanish colonial government. Martí replied, "Tell the General that Martí is not the kind of man that can be bought."[5]

Martí was again deported to Spain. His wife, who disapproved of his revolutionary views, chose to stay in Cuba with their infant son. Martí's marriage was failing, but he did not allow this to deter him from his activities in behalf of Cuba's independence. This time, he stayed in Spain only a few months and then simply walked away. He went to France, and from there he took a boat to New York. From now on, New York was to be his base. He would not return to Cuba until he felt that the time was ripe for revolution.

LIVING BY
HIS PEN

Martí arrived in New York on January 3, 1880. The first thing he did was get in touch with the Cuban community of rebels in exile. He became a member of the Cuban Revolutionary Committee and immediately began writing, lecturing, and teaching on behalf of the revolution. From the beginning, he attempted to bring all the separate parties together and unite them under one banner.

By September 1880, it had become obvious that the Little War was over. Martí and other officials of the Revolutionary Committee wrote to the few elements of the revolutionary army that were still fighting and urged them to lay down their arms. It was useless for them to continue. It would be better to regroup and prepare for the future struggle, which Martí was sure was coming. The Revolutionary Committee was disbanded, and Martí was forced to take stock of his situation. The outlook was not good.

Carmen joined Martí in New York for a while, but they quarreled about his commitment to the coming revolution. Carmen even admitted that she was quite content to live under Spanish rule. She returned to Cuba with her son in January 1881, leaving Martí alone in New York. Martí was not the single-minded revolutionary he appeared to be. He cared for his family, especially his son, José, for whom he wrote his first book of verse, *Ismaelillo* (Little Ishmael). In fifteen poems, he describes the anguish he feels at being separated from his son. Martí's intense desire to be reunited with his son can also be seen as his longing for a return to Cuba, from which he had been separated for so long. He also attempts to pass on to his son a moral code to guide him in the path to virtue. The great Nicaraguan poet Rubén Darío called *Ismaelillo* a guide to the art of being a father.[1]

With *Ismaelillo*, Martí also broke new ground as a poet. He knew that he was doing something

Martí dedicated his first book of poems, *Ismaelillo*, to his son, José.

different. In his dedication to his son, he says, "If someone should tell you that these pages resemble others, tell him I love you too much to thus dishonor you. I depict you just as my eyes have seen you."[2] The simplicity of the verses are a far cry from the flowery style of the Spanish Romantic poets. The book has been recognized by literary historians as the first example of the Modernist movement in Latin American literature. This movement in poetry was noted for turning its back on traditional methods and using new forms and meters. It used everyday language and was not restricted to the use of rhyme. *Ismaelillo* became a landmark in the history of Latin American poetry.

With the end of the Revolutionary Committee in New York, Martí no longer had a base from which to continue his crusade for independence, and he had to make a living. He again took up his pen, but this time to write of more general things, such as his observations and feelings about the United States. One of his first published pieces, called "Impressions of America," appeared in the magazine *Hour*. This led to a series that became a feature of the magazine. He also began writing articles for *The New York Sun*. The editor of the *Sun* was Charles A. Dana, who became Martí's friend and a faithful supporter in the years to come. Martí wrote articles for all of the

Spanish-language publications in New York, and he even had time to edit a magazine, *La Edad de Oro* (The Golden Age), for Spanish-speaking children. He even wrote a novel, *Amistad funesta* (Sad Friendship), under an assumed name. This took him only seven days, and his haste must have shown, because it received some very bad reviews. One critic wrote that it was "dull, diffuse, if not artificial and false."[3] It has some interest, though, because the hero, Juan Jerez, embodies so many of the feelings and personal circumstances of Martí himself:

> He traveled because he was full of eagles, which gnawed at his body, and wanted wide spaces, and were suffocating in the prison of the city. He traveled because he was married to a woman whom he thought he had loved, and whom he then found like an insensible cup, in which the harmonies of his soul found no echo.[4]

In 1887, Martí discovered a book that seemed to mirror his own feelings about the injustice done to the native Indian population of Mexico. It was Helen Hunt Jackson's *Ramona,* and the fact that it was written by a North American interested Martí. He wrote: "Our race . . . [is] recognized in all of its goodness by a famous writer among those who have most disdained us."[5] Martí was stretching the truth a little here because he could hardly be

The first edition of *La Edad de Oro (The Age of Gold),* a monthly magazine for children published and edited by Martí, was dedicated to "the children of America."

considered a Mexican Indian. He translated the book into Spanish and published it at his own expense. Most critics consider his translation far superior in style to the original novel.

Martí published two more books of poetry during his lifetime, *Versos libres* (Free Verses) and *Versos sencillos* (Simple Verses). The word "free" in the title of the first has two meanings. In one sense, it refers both to the form (which follows various rhyme schemes or none at all) and to the variety of the subject matter. The second meaning is the simple political freedom that Martí sought in all his writings and speeches. *Versos sencillos* was written in the Catskill mountains of New York State, where Martí had gone for health reasons and for a long-needed rest. The poems are very personal, reflecting Martí's own experiences and feelings. It contains many of his best-known poems.

Martí was now so well-known throughout the Latin American world that he was offered a teaching post in Venezuela. On March 21, 1881, he left New York for Caracas, where he hoped to renew his efforts on behalf of Cuban independence. He founded a magazine, *La Revista Venezolana* (The Venezuelan Review), but it lasted for only two issues. As usual, Martí had offended the authorities by writing an article in praise of a writer who was a political outcast in Venezuela. Martí thought it wise to return to New York. He continued to write articles for Venezuelan newspapers, but they were mostly articles on literary and artistic subjects.

During these early years in the United States, Martí was one of the busiest men in New York. He always wore black suits and a black tie, and he was a familiar figure as he dashed from newspaper offices to printers, to publishers, and to meetings and lectures. He reviewed books and plays and reported on public events, such as the opening of the Brooklyn Bridge in 1883 and the dedication of the Statue of Liberty in 1886. He translated books from Spanish to English for the American publisher D. Appleton and Company, and he began to write in English for journals and newspapers. He also worked as a translator and assistant in the office of a prominent New York businessman. Perhaps the clerical and accounting skills he acquired as a boy working for his father helped him in this area. In 1883, he became the editor of a business magazine, *La América*, which showed that he was a practical man of affairs and not just a poet and revolutionary.

Martí wrote articles, essays, and newsletters for newspapers and journals in Argentina, Colombia, Honduras, Mexico, Paraguay, Uruguay, and Venezuela. He thus became the number one interpreter of the United States for Latin America. In 1884, he was appointed vice-consul for Uruguay in New York. Later, he was appointed consul for Argentina and Paraguay. So the title of diplomat was added to his list of achievements.

At first, Martí was delighted with the United States. He was fascinated by a country "where everyone looks like his own master. One can breathe freely, freedom being here the foundation, the shield, the essence of life."[6] In his "Impressions of America," written for the magazine *Hour*, he wrote:

> Here, one can be proud of the species. Everybody works. Everybody reads. . . . I feel obligated to this country, where the unprotected always find a friend. . . . Here, a good idea always finds welcoming, soft, and fertile ground. One must be intelligent, that is all. Do something useful, and you will have everything you want.[7]

Martí's early New York writings are filled with such praise. He was used to the world of Cuba and Spain, with its strict social classes, its domination by the church and state, its oppression of the lowly, and its resistance to new ideas and change. The United States for him was truly a land where the common people had "at last won Glory."[8]

Martí was especially impressed with American writers. In essay after essay, he provided his Spanish-speaking readers with accounts of the lives and works of North America's greatest poets, novelists, and essayists of that time. In so doing, he played an important part in the cultural history of Latin America. Thanks to Martí's influence, future Latin American writers were to look to other countries and cultures in addition to Europe for their inspiration and example. Modern writers such as Gabriel García Márquez speak of the "North American masters" as their literary forebears.[9] If it had not been for Martí, Latin American writers might have followed the academic tradition of imitating European models that were quite different from the new societies of South and Central America.

Martí introduced his readers to Ralph Waldo Emerson, Henry Wadsworth Longfellow, John Greenleaf Whittier, Mark Twain, and Louisa May Alcott. He also discussed Edgar Allen Poe, James Russell Lowell, Washington Irving, Henry David Thoreau, Nathaniel Hawthorne, and many more. His essays were not just biographical sketches but in-depth discussions of his subjects' work. Martí's article on Ralph Waldo Emerson has been called one of the best essays ever written in Spanish and is a good example of Martí's scholarship and artistic opinions.[10] Martí was fascinated by Emerson and considered him a giant among writers. He admired the writer both for his independent thought and for his belief that the poet was closer to truth than was the scientist or philosopher. In fact, he called Emerson "the Philosopher of Democracy."[11] Another of his favorites was Mark Twain. He described *A Connecticut Yankee in King Arthur's Court* as a "fight, cowboy style, with a lasso and gun"[12] against all the oppression and injustice in life.

He was also especially interested in Wendell Phillips and Henry Ward Beecher, whose lifelong battles against slavery were so much like Martí's struggles. As a poet, Martí was drawn to Walt Whitman, whom he considered a natural poet who scorned the formal manners and methods of traditional poets. In his own poetry, Martí was doing the same thing, introducing a new voice into the stilted and flowery language of traditional Spanish literature.

Martí's admiration for the United States began to wane, however, shortly after he began his "Impressions of America" series. He could not help noticing the great differences among the various New York social classes. On the one hand, there were the wealthy families of Fifth Avenue and upper Manhattan. On the other hand, there were the wretched poor of the Bowery and the Lower East Side. To Martí, this gap between the

This illustration from *Harper's Weekly* shows Printing House Square, just southeast of City Hall. In the center is *The New York Times* building, next to it is *The New York Herald*, and to the left of that *The New York Sun*, for which Martí wrote many articles.

haves and the have-nots seemed almost criminal in a nation as wealthy as the United States.

Martí reported and commented on the political scene in New York City for his Spanish-speaking readers. He soon became aware of the machine politicians, who were the true legislators of the city and state and even of the nation. He wrote that the whole system was built on bribery and corruption, a situation that was completely at odds with the democratic system he had so admired. He had thought that the Spanish colonial system was as corrupt as any could be, but the situation in New York seemed just as bad.

Martí had always admired the small farmers and working men of Cuba. He felt that all that was needed for their happiness and prosperity was popular democracy under an independent government. At first, he believed that this had been achieved in the United States. But, this was a period of rapid change in the United States. The nation was becoming completely industrialized, and the means of production of goods became more and more centered in a few large corporations. The small farmers and independent businessmen and manufacturers whom Martí credited with the industriousness and energy of the country were fast losing out to mammoth industrialists.

Martí also noted the tensions between the North and the South following the Civil War in America. The freed slaves, many of whom had traveled north to join an already large immigrant population, were angry that they were not being given the freedom and equality they had been promised. Thousands upon thousands of immigrants had poured into the United States to fill the needs of the new industrialized society. Martí saw them as motivated by greed rather than the need to partake of the freedom they had been denied in their native countries. This mixture of races and nationalities had produced an atmosphere of intolerance and bigotry, the one thing that Martí had most deplored in Cuba and Latin America.

Martí sensed that the United States, with all its power and energy, was embarking on a program of domination of the Western Hemisphere. Cuba was dependent upon the United States as the principal market for its most important export—sugar. After the Ten Years War, many North American companies had purchased sugar plantations and refineries from Cuban Criollos who had been bankrupted by the war. The presence and influence of the United States was increasing yearly in Cuba, and there was now renewed talk of Cuba becoming a state. Martí believed that this would be a disaster for Cuba, and he warned his readers of it repeatedly in his writings. He also hoped that Cuba could learn from what was happening in the United States and avoid making the same mistakes. What he wanted was a completely independent Cuba, free to pursue its own destiny in harmony and peace.

Martí was later to write of his fears of domination of Cuba by the United States, "I have lived in the monster and I know its entrails."[13]

WORKING FOR
THE REVOLUTION

Martí had many things with which to occupy himself during his early years in New York, but he never forgot the cause for which he had decided to devote his life. In 1884, he was given the chance to renew his efforts for Cuban independence.

General Máximo Gómez, one of the heroes of the Ten Years War, was furious at the way the Treaty of Zanjón had been all but ignored by the Spanish government. He decided to gather his forces together to renew the military struggle against Spain. He journeyed from his home in

Santo Domingo to Honduras to meet with Antonio Maceo, the courageous general who had refused to acknowledge the end of the war. The two of them communicated with Cuban exiles and émigrés in the United States and learned that the revolutionary spirit still existed there. Together, they journeyed to New York to meet with members of the Cuban communities with the aim of raising funds to support an invasion of the island.

Martí had earlier written to the two generals to introduce himself and to convince them that the revolution had not died and that he was eager to pursue its goals. Gómez and Maceo met with Martí and were impressed with the young man's devotion to the Cuban cause. Gómez appointed Maceo and Martí heads of a mission to visit Cuban communities in the United States to raise funds for the coming struggle, but when Martí outlined some of his plans for the financing and conduct of the invasion, Gómez rebuked him, telling him to follow orders and let Maceo take care of the planning. This made Martí, who was already distrustful of the military, wary of Gómez and Maceo. He felt that they considered the revolution their own personal property and were not likely to put any postwar government in the hands of civilians.

Consequently, on October 20, 1884, Martí resigned from the movement. He gave as his

José Martí and General Máximo Gómez met in New York in 1884 to discuss the aims of the Cuban Revolutionary Party.

reason that he could not see the point of "planning to plunge a nation into war only to take possession of that nation at some later date."[1] From that date on, Martí was totally opposed to any form of military government for Cuba.

In 1889, Martí turned to rallying his fellow exiles against the possible takeover of Cuba by the United States. James G. Blaine, U.S. secretary of state under President Benjamin Harrison, saw Cuba as a valuable addition to United States territory. It was a ready supplier of sugar, and its position in the Caribbean Sea made it a valuable stronghold for defense of Central America and Mexico. There was also talk of building a canal across Panama to connect the Atlantic and Pacific oceans. Such a canal would make Cuba's position in the Caribbean Sea even more important as a defensive position. Members of Congress were predicting that in the near future the United States would possess the whole of the North American continent, from Canada to Central America. Martí had seen what happened to the United States as a result of the freeing of its slaves, a flood of immigrants, and the rise of big business. He feared that Cuba, with its large slave and freed-slave population, would fall victim to the intolerance and bigotry that had overtaken the United States. Also, with its economy based on a single resource, sugar, Cuba would be easy prey for the large corporations then gobbling up all the resources of the United States.

Not everyone in the United States was in favor of annexing Cuba, and for the worst reasons. In 1889, *The Philadelphia Manufacturer* published an editorial in which it asked, "Do We Want Cuba?" It argued that the island's population of impoverished Cuban Criollos, corrupt Spaniards, and freed slaves was not capable of functioning in a government such as that of the United States. To give such people the same elective power as "the freemen of our Northern States would be to summon them to the performance of functions for which they have not the slightest capacity."[2] In other words, they were inferior.

Martí, quick to react to this insult, wrote a forceful reply, "Vindication of Cuba," which was published in *The New York Evening Post.* In it, he defended Cuban culture as the product of a civilized and knowledgeable society. He also cited the bravery of the Cuban population in rebelling against a corrupt and unjust system as an indication of a political awareness equal to that of the average citizen of the United States. He went so far as to say that no Cuban would agree to become part of a country so self-centered and so confident of its superiority.[3] Martí made plans to publish a newspaper, written in English, which would answer any future slurs against his country. He wrote, "What I want is to demonstrate that we are good people, industrious and capable."[4]

This affair served to renew Martí's activity in the independence movement. From October 1889 to April 1890, the first Pan-American Conference was held in Washington, D.C. This was dominated by Secretary of State James G. Blaine, who tried to convince Latin American countries to open their borders to American commerce and investment. Martí saw it as one more attempt by the United States to increase its influence in Latin America. Martí made a speech in which he urged the delegates to declare their "second independence," this time from the United States.[5]

In 1891, Martí attended the Inter-American Monetary Conference as the Uruguayan delegate. The United States used the conference to again try to open up Latin America to its economic interests and to back all American currencies with both silver and gold. Until then, most currencies in the Western Hemisphere were backed by gold, but silver-producing nations such as the United States, Mexico, and Peru urged that silver be given an equal status with gold. Martí again made a speech in which he pointed out that since most Central and South American countries produced little or no silver, the new standard would not do them any good and, indeed, might weaken their currencies. The proposal was turned down by the delegates, and Martí was given credit for defeating the designs of the U.S. Department of State.

Martí's prominent place in all of these negotiations led to complaints in diplomatic circles. It was pointed out that it was hardly proper for a Cuban revolutionary to represent another country at an international conference. Martí heard of this and resigned from all of his diplomatic positions. From this point on, he devoted himself exclusively to the struggle for Cuban independence.

Martí now decided to take the lead in the independence movement. He allied himself with the African-Cuban segments of the émigré community by helping them establish an educational institution, *La Liga* (The League), for African Cubans. He knew that he would have to have the support of African Cubans and the poor farmers and laborers, who formed the majority of the Cuban population. Working-class Cuban émigrés were found mostly in Florida, and they worked in the Cuban-owned cigar factories of Tampa and Key West. Florida had always been the center of Cuban settlement in the United States for an obvious reason: It was only ninety miles from the Cuban mainland.

From 1887 until 1895, Martí met with any group that
would lend support and money for the revolutionary cause.
Here he poses with a group of wealthy Cuban émigré
businessmen in Florida.

The Cuban cigar-making industry, quite liberal
for the times, provided good working conditions
and services, such as reading rooms and meeting
places, for employees. The factories employed
people whose only duty was to read aloud from
newspapers and periodicals while the cigar rollers
worked at their humdrum tasks. The reading
material dealt mostly with news of the war for

independence, the political scene in Cuba, and articles on cultural and social affairs. Since Martí was the number one contributor to such periodicals, his name was known to practically every Cuban in Florida.

In November of 1891, Martí was in Tampa, Florida. He was there at the invitation of a Cuban patriotic club to deliver an address to the members. On November 26, Martí made his famous "Liceo" speech, named after the Cuban Lyceum, the building where the meeting was held. In this speech, Martí outlined his vision of what Cuba could be, a land of racial harmony and justice for all. He said that "Cuba must be taken as an altar, to offer our lives on it." His motto was the title of the speech: "Everyone Together and for the Well-Being of All."[6] At the end of the speech, the audience rushed the stage and swamped him with hugs and handshakes. They put him on their shoulders and carried him through the streets of Tampa, shouting patriotic slogans and singing the Cuban national anthem.

The next day, Martí gave another speech, this one in remembrance of eight medical students who had been executed in Havana twenty years earlier. In the speech, he did not lament the death of the students but, rather, said that sometimes he saw death as necessary, as the "pillow, as the

yeast, as the triumph of life."[7] He urged the crowd
to rise to the heroism and sacrifice that would be
needed to gain the long-desired and fought-for
independence of Cuba. The speech was greeted
with as much enthusiasm as his speech of the day
before. The two speeches were printed in a
pamphlet that was distributed throughout Cuban
communities in Florida. No doubt they were read
aloud to the workers in the cigar-making factories.

Martí was made a member of the Cuban
Patriotic League of Tampa. He met with its
members and with a delegation of workers to draft
a statement of the aims of the revolutionary
movement. They drew up two documents now
known as the *Tampa Resolutions* and the *Bases of
the Cuban Revolutionary Party*. There is little doubt
that these two documents were written primarily
by Martí. In them, he set forth the organization of
the party, which would consist of all the local
social and revolutionary clubs. It would collect
funds, encourage its friends in Cuba to follow a
revolutionary course, and establish relations with
other revolutionary movements throughout Latin
America.

When Martí returned to New York, he took
steps to include all the New York clubs in the party
he was forming. His next move was to contact the
various clubs and revolutionary organizations in

Key West, Florida. The Key West revolutionaries were much more active than those in the rest of the United States, and they had actually built up an underground system in Cuba itself. Martí knew that such an organization was crucial to his plans, so he set about winning over Key West Cubans to his side. Rather than replace their organizations with his own, he sought to join them, and thus present a united front to the Spanish colonial government.

Martí visited Key West on December 26, 1891, and met with all the leaders of the patriotic and revolutionary clubs. Because he was in ill health, he was unable to speak to the assembled revolutionaries. On January 5, 1892, he was at least able to read the *Tampa Resolutions* and the *Bases of the Cuban Revolutionary Party* to all the delegates. These were unanimously accepted, and the congratulations and celebrations that followed made it obvious to everyone that José Martí was the real leader of the Cuban movement for independence.

Martí returned to New York and, on March 14, 1892, published the first issue of a new Spanish-language newspaper named *Patria*. This paper became the official voice of the revolutionary movement. Martí, of course, was its editor; in its pages he urged other Cuban communities to issue their own newspapers in order to keep the revolutionary spirit alive.

The Cuban Revolutionary Party's existence was formally announced on April 10, 1892. All Cuban and Puerto Rican patriotic organizations and clubs were included in the new party. For the first time, all Spanish-speaking émigrés and exiles were united in the pursuit of one aim, the independence of Cuba from Spain. Martí was designated the official delegate of the body, which meant that for all practical purposes he was the president.

The final aim of the revolutionary party was to promote a revolt inside Cuba while at the same time invading it with a military force from the outside. In order to do this, Martí had to have the support and cooperation of military veterans of the Ten Years War. Most of the officers of the rebel army were in exile in various countries in Latin America. Many of them had remained active plotters against Spain and were anxious to renew the war against that country. They all had their separate followers and their separate plans for renewing the struggle. It was now Martí's task to unite them under one organization, the Cuban Revolutionary Party.

Everyone in the party agreed that the leader of the military wing had to be General Máximo Gómez, who was still considered a hero by most Cubans. Martí and Gómez had broken off relations eight years previously, in 1884. Now, however, Martí felt that it was time for them to forget their differences and unite in the task ahead. Martí and General Gómez exchanged friendly letters, with the result that Martí visited Gómez in the Dominican Republic. Their meeting took place at Gómez's ranch at Montecristi, near the capital city of Santo Domingo. The two men came to what has been called the *Agreement of Montecristi*. This document announced that the Cuban Revolutionary Party would devote itself to preparing for the war and that the war would be conducted by General Gómez as commander-in-chief.

Martí next went to Costa Rica, where he met with the other hero of the Ten Years War, General Antonio Maceo. Martí also had to do some fence-mending with Maceo, with whom he had also broken off relations in 1884. Martí convinced a reluctant Maceo, who was prospering as a landowner and farmer in Costa Rica, to join the party and serve as Gómez's field general.

Martí now turned all his energies toward raising funds and solidifying the authority of the Cuban Revolutionary Party throughout the United States, the Caribbean, and Central America. He traveled widely in all three areas, giving speeches, appointing or backing local representatives to the party, and generally strengthening the party's organization.

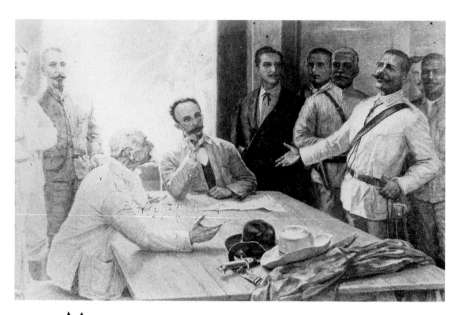

Martí met with General Antonio Maceo and listened to his views about the future of the Cuban government. Unfortunately, they often disagreed.

One of his main objectives was to build an underground network in Cuba itself that would recognize and take direction from the party. To this end, he sent emissaries to Cuba to make contact with all the rebel groups on the island and to try to join them all in a united front.

Raising money was a problem. The wealthy landowners in Cuba and the Cuban manufacturers and businessmen in the émigré communities were still reluctant to break away completely from Spain. They believed that self-government under Spanish rule was still the best course to follow.

Martí, of course, believed that complete independence was the only answer to Cuba's problems. So he turned to the working people of the Cuban communities, and they responded by contributing willingly to the party's cause. The tobacco workers of Tampa and Key West contributed a day's pay each week!

Unfortunately, the United States suffered an economic depression in 1884, and it had a severe effect on the cigar-making industry in this country. Many Cubans lost their jobs and were forced to move to other parts of the United States in search of work. Strikes among the remaining workers in Key West further disrupted Martí's influence there and he was in danger of losing an important power base. The economic situation gradually improved, but not many people had confidence in its stability. Martí decided to act while the party was still an active force in Cuban revolutionary affairs.

REVOLUTION

In April of 1894, General Gómez came to New York and met with Martí to plan the invasion of Cuba. Their plan was that there would be a general uprising by the underground revolutionary forces in Cuba at the same time that Gómez was invading the eastern part of the island with a force of about two hundred Cubans and Dominicans. Antonio Maceo would launch an invasion from Costa Rica to land in Oriente province. A third expedition would leave from Key West and land at Camagüey province, in the central part of the island.

By late December of 1894, everything was ready. Three fast ships were rented and made ready for the upcoming invasions. The three ships were to leave from Fernandina Harbor, not far from Jacksonville, Florida. The captains of the ships had been told that their destination was Central America. Once at sea, the Cubans planned to force the captains to follow their plan for the landings in Cuba. One ship was to go first to Costa Rica to pick up Antonio Maceo and his men and then invade Cuba from the north. Martí and his men would sail first to the Dominican Republic to meet with Gómez and his volunteers so that they could invade Cuba from the south. The third ship would go first to Key West and there pick up the remaining invading force to land at Camagüey province.

The "Fernandina Filibuster," as the plan was called, suddenly fell apart. A member of the Cuban Revolutionary Party accidentally revealed the plan to one of the captains of the ships, who spread it among the waterfronts of Florida. The Spanish government soon heard the rumors and made a complaint to the State Department in Washington, D.C. The United States government could hardly condone an invasion of a foreign country starting from its own shores, so it seized the three ships and all of the arms on board. Martí managed to escape to New York, but most of the men on board were arrested.

Much to Martí's surprise, the failure of the "Fernandina Filibuster" did not mark the end of the Cuban Revolutionary Party. Instead, the émigré communities rallied to his support. One wealthy Cuban woman offered to put up bail for all of the men who were arrested. An American lawyer, Horatio S. Rubens, who had assisted Martí during the strikes in Key West, managed to save some of the supplies from the ships. But most important, the plan convinced the wealthy members of the Cuban community in Florida and New York that Martí was serious about his intentions to wage a revolutionary war against Spain. The slight, idealistic poet became a hero and an idol to exiled Cubans throughout the Americas. Cigar makers and businesspeople began to send money and lend their full support to the Cuban Revolutionary Party. In many ways, the "Fernandina Filibuster" was a victory for Martí.

Revolutionary fever swept through Cuba and the émigré communities. All the military leaders and veterans of the Ten Years War offered Martí their services. Martí was quick to respond to this new wave of enthusiasm for an invasion. On January 29, 1895, Martí, Gómez, and an official representative of the Cuban Revolutionary Party issued an order for the revolution in Cuba to begin. Juan Gualberto Gómez, who represented the party in Havana, was told to set a date for a popular uprising whenever he thought that the two provinces of Oriente and Camagüey could support a military invasion.

Martí traveled from New York to the Dominican Republic to join General Gómez and work out the plans for the invasion. He arrived at Montecristi on February 7 and there awaited word from Cuba that the uprising had begun. Unfortunately, Martí's concentration on the invasion was broken when word arrived that Antonio Maceo was balking at joining the operation. Maceo gave as his excuse that he was not given a large enough share of the party's funds to finance his end of the invasion. Actually, he had lost faith in Martí, doubting that the younger man could carry off such a grand enterprise. Martí wrote him a sharp letter to pull him into line. Maceo finally agreed to join in the invasion, but he never recognized Martí as the real leader of the revolution.

On February 24, 1895, the *"Grito de Baire"* ("Cry from Baire") was made from within Cuba, and the uprising began. Unfortunately, Spanish spies had known all along that the uprising was going to take place, and they immediately arrested all of the revolutionary leaders in Havana. The revolt in the western provinces was put down by the Spanish almost before it began, so the revolution was confined to the eastern provinces.

When Martí learned of the spread of the revolution in Oriente province, he drafted a message to the Cuban people called *El Manifiesto de Montecristi* (The Manifesto of Montecristi). In it, he justified the revolution and put forth its aims. He also enlarged upon his ideas for the future. He saw Cuba as an independent republic, completely free from any outside influences or military control. He saw an end to Cuba's one-crop economy and its domination by the United States. He saw an end to racial discrimination and appreciation, rather than fear, of Cuba's African population. Martí and Gómez signed the manifesto on March 25, 1895. On the very same day, Martí wrote to a friend in the Dominican Republic: "I promoted the war; with it my responsibility begins, not ends."[1]

Many of Martí's followers thought that he should return to New York and oversee the efforts of the Cuban Revolutionary Party to support the revolution. Martí stoutly refused. He wrote in his "political will" that he was "dying of shame" at the thought that he had asked others to give their lives for a cause he was unwilling to risk his life for.[2] He

José Martí in Jamaica in 1892. He is wearing his usual outfit, a black suit with simple white shirt and black tie.

addressed this will to his friend Federico Henríquez, a prominent citizen of the Dominican Republic. He also wrote a "literary will," in which he directed that all of his papers and manuscripts should go to his friend Gonzalo de Quesada, whom he appointed his editor. This concern with wills and his work indicated that Martí was deadly serious about what he was going to undertake. This was no mere idealistic adventure he was setting out on. The invasion of Cuba was the end and purpose of his life, and he was willing to die for it.

Before he left Montecristi, Martí wrote a poem of farewell. It was to be his last poem.

Adiós. El vapor irá
En la semana que viene:
Ya lo tiene, ya lo tiene
Un amigo que se va.

Yo de mí le he de decir
Que en seguirlo, sereno,
Sin miedo al rayo ni al trueno
Elaboro el porvenir

Su
José Martí [3]

(Goodbye. The ship leaves
In the coming week.
Now you have, now you hold
A friend who is leaving.

And of me I have to say
That in following it, serenely,
Without fear of the lightning or the thunder
I am working out the future

Yours
José Martí)

On April 1, 1895, the same day that he wrote his literary will, Martí set out with Gómez and four other men for Inagua, a town on the coast of the Dominican Republic. They had already hired a ship to take them to Cuba, but when they arrived in Inagua, they could not find either the ship or its captain. A German freighter, the *Nordstand*, was in the harbor, bound for Haiti with a cargo of fruit. Martí gave the captain a $1,000 bribe to take him and his party aboard and drop them off in a small boat near the coast of Cuba. On the night of April 1, 1895, Martí and Gómez, together with three Cubans and one Dominican, boarded the vessel and hid below decks. These four men were a far cry from the two hundred men that Martí and Gómez were supposed to have raised for their part of the invasion. However, it was too late to turn back, and Martí's presence in Cuba was more important to the cause than a thousand men would be. After some mix-ups and delays, the ship finally took to sea; and on April 10, it arrived three miles off the coast of Cuba at Cape Maisí.

The six men put their weapons and provisions in a small rowboat and then climbed in themselves. The weather was bad and the boat overloaded, so they had trouble maneuvering the boat to shore. Spanish patrol boats were in the vicinity, so they could not make any noise or show a light. Martí wrote in his diary:

> We strap on our revolvers. Head toward clearing. Moon comes up red from behind a cloud. We land on a stony beach, La Playita (at foot of Cabobajo). I the last to leave the boat, bailing it out. Jump ashore. Great joy. . . . Sleep on the ground nearby.[4]

The following day, they broke camp and headed inland. Martí had come home at last.

Antonio Maceo had already landed in Oriente province. His group had then made their way on foot to Guantánamo, in southeastern Cuba, through rough country. In order to avoid detection by Spanish troops in the area, Maceo had split his small force into even smaller groups. Martí and Gómez met one of these groups, and hearing that Maceo was in the area, pressed on in hopes of meeting him. With their forces united, they could try to contact the underground groups and rebels who had been fighting the Spanish for more than a month. As they progressed inland, they picked up volunteers and sympathizers with their cause along the way. They also learned from friendly farmers that they were being followed by Spanish army units.

On April 15, Gómez surprised Martí by promoting him to major general of what they called the Liberation Army. Of course, this was more a recognition of Martí's importance to the revolution than of his military abilities, but Martí was still pleased and proud. He wrote in his diary: "Up until today I have not felt that I was a man. I have lived ashamed and have dragged the chain of my fatherland all of my life."[5] Now he felt that he was a soldier, marching with his comrades to do battle, with the "jubilation with which men offer themselves for sacrifice."[6]

The invasion force continued westward until it reached the area of Guantánamo. Here they learned that Maceo was operating in the vicinity of Santiago de Cuba, the largest city in eastern Cuba. Maceo, who was perhaps the most popular of the heroes of the Ten Years War, had attracted an army of six thousand volunteers. Martí and Gómez hastened to join Maceo. It was while still marching over rough country that Martí was interviewed by a correspondent for the *The New York Herald,* George E. Bryson. Although the last thing Martí wanted was for the United States to become involved in the revolution, he realized that he must convince the American public of the rightness of his cause. This would at least make it difficult for the United States government to side with Spain. He therefore sent a letter to the editor of the *Herald* outlining his plans for the revolution and the future government of Cuba.

This matter of the future of Cuba caused differences between Martí and Maceo when their forces finally met. It was May 5, 1895, when Martí and Gómez joined Maceo in a village near Santiago de Cuba. They immediately began to plan their future strategy. They agreed that the war must be spread as quickly as possible to the western part of the island. Maceo tried to get Martí to return to the United States to coordinate efforts to supply the revolutionary forces. Martí refused, insisting that he was needed in Cuba. Martí and Maceo also disagreed on what was to happen after the revolution succeeded.

Martí had always insisted that the government of Cuba be a republic, firmly in the hands of civilian representatives who would make all decisions democratically. Maceo was in favor of a military *junta,* a small group of army officers who would steer the new nation through its first difficult years. Martí knew from his experience in Mexico and Central America that a junta tends to remain in power long after the nation has been established.

This he wanted to avoid at all costs, even more than he wanted to avoid the interference of foreign powers in Cuba's internal affairs. Maceo stubbornly refused to bend to Martí's wishes. He was so displeased that he refused to let Martí and Gómez review his troops. He relented the following day, however, and Martí was allowed to speak to the army. He promised them that there would be no surrender of the revolutionary forces until complete and absolute independence had been assured.

That same day, May 6, Martí and Gómez's small force resumed its march westward until, on May 12, they arrived at Dos Ríos, a small town on the Cauto river in the foothills of the Contramaestre mountains. Here they made their camp, and Martí resumed his never-ending task of writing dispatches to the various revolutionary groups, appeals for support from émigré groups abroad, and personal letters to people in high places as well as to friends.

On May 17, Gómez learned from scouts and the friendly population of the area that a large Spanish force was in the vicinity. He left immediately with a large number of men to scout and harass the enemy and possibly engage in battle. Martí was left in camp, suffering from the long-term effects of the injury he had received in prison during his captivity as a youth. On May 18, he began a

Martí poses with a group of Cuban revolutionaries in Central America. He was at home in a jungle hut as well as in a businessman's office.

letter to Manuel Mercado, the family friend who had gotten him his first job in Mexico and with whom he had kept up a lifelong correspondence. In this letter, he repeated his dreams of democracy for Cuba, for racial and social harmony, and for freedom from outside influences. He wrote that it was his duty "to prevent, by the independence of Cuba, the United States from spreading over the West Indies and falling with that added weight upon other lands of our America."[7]

"Our America" was a phrase that Martí had been using more and more in his writings and speeches. It was his one overpowering concern, and he had served it at the expense of his health, his family, and his personal life.

The letter to Mercado was never finished. The next day, when he heard the sounds of a nearby battle, he could not bear to remain in camp while others were fighting and dying for a cause he so strongly believed in. He therefore disobeyed orders by leaping on a white horse and riding headlong into the fray. He was recognized by Spanish soldiers and died in a hail of bullets.

THE WAR
AND AFTER

The death of Martí dealt a terrible blow to the revolutionary cause and was a tragedy for the Cuban people. The war went on, however; and Gómez and Maceo continued their guerrilla tactics until they had reached the western part of Cuba. They scored some decisive victories over the Spanish army and, within little more than a year, were in control of almost the whole of the Cuban countryside. The Spanish were still in control of the large cities and key strongholds, but they were in a virtual state of siege. Antonio Maceo was about to attack Havana itself when he was killed in action on December 7, 1896. The Spanish army still outnumbered the rebels by about five to one, but the morale of the Spanish soldiers was low; after all, they were fighting far from home and under terrible conditions. Many of them died of disease, and all of them felt the hostility of the local populations, most of whom were on the side of the rebels.

Meanwhile, the political leadership of the revolution had passed into the hands of Tómas Estrada Palma, a distinguished Cuban exile in New York who had helped Martí organize the Cuban Revolutionary Party. Estrada Palma had always favored closer ties with the United States, and he had even moved the headquarters of the party to Washington, D.C., to be closer to the people he hoped to win over to the side of Cuba. In fact, he spent more time lobbying in the United States Congress than he did raising funds and supplies to support the revolution.

Estrada Palma's actions did not go over well with the rebel army. The army was composed primarily of poor farmers and former slaves—who wanted to be part of the postwar government—but their officers were in favor of a military junta. The people in favor of the republic that Martí had worked so hard to see established favored a democratically elected civilian government. So the revolutionaries were hopelessly divided, and there was no one with Martí's skills and reputation to bring them together. Although the Liberation Army was now in reach of its goals, it was still desperately in need of arms and supplies to deliver the final blow that would defeat the Spanish army. At this point, the United States came forward to deliver the means of striking that final blow.

From the beginning of the Second War of Cuban Independence, as it was then called, the United States had refrained from recognizing Cuba's right to independence. Presidents Grover Cleveland and William McKinley favored Spain in the struggle because they thought that Spanish rule was best for American commercial interests. Most of the Cuban sugar industry was now in the hands of United States citizens, and Spain treated them most favorably.

However, now that it appeared that Spain was losing the war, President McKinley decided to step in to protect United States interests and to assure their preservation in an independent Cuba. The United States could have simply annexed Cuba, putting it directly under its control. This would have suited Estrada Palma and his Cuban Revolutionary Party. The trouble with this tactic was that the United States would have had to face the Liberation Army, which could mean a brand-new war. The United States, therefore, decided to withdraw its support of Spain and not to annex Cuba. Its new policy was to help the revolutionaries by giving them aid and encouragement.

Then, on February 15, 1898, the United States battleship *Maine* blew up in Havana harbor, killing 260 people on board. The cause of the explosion remains a mystery, but the United States blamed it on Spain. American public opinion, which had already been largely pro-Cuban, turned violently anti-Spain. McKinley promptly recognized the independence of Cuba, demanding that Spain withdraw completely from the island. Spain of course refused, and McKinley asked Congress for a declaration of war, which was granted on April 25, 1898.

The Spanish-American War, as it is now called, lasted only three months. Spain was forced to surrender in the face of overwhelming American forces, particularly on the sea. Practically the entire Spanish fleet was destroyed in the harbor of Manila, Philippine Islands, and in the harbor of Santiago de Cuba. There was some heavy fighting on land, most notably at San Juan Hill, where Theodore Roosevelt gained fame by leading his Rough Riders in a charge up the hill. The United States government dealt directly with the Spanish government during the peace negotiations, as though the Cuban Liberation Army had not existed. The United States has always taken credit for the defeat of the Spanish forces and the liberation of Cuba, which Cuban patriots stoutly deny. They feel strongly that Cuba was freed from Spanish domination by Cubans themselves, and not by the Yankees from the north.

The United States occupied Cuba for four years, from 1898 to 1902. The Cuban Revolutionary Party was no longer needed, and the Liberation Army ceased to exist. The new government that Martí had envisioned was never formed, and the United States took over all government and commercial functions. The wealthy landowners were restored to their old positions in the social and economic order of Cuba, and United States corporations were given generous trading rights. In short, everything that Martí had feared came to pass.

Before ending the occupation and leaving the island, the United States forced the new Cuban assembly to adopt the Platt Amendment to its new constitution. This amendment was named after United States Senator Orville Platt, who proposed that the United States had the right to supervise the Cuban government and to intervene in its affairs if it felt justified in doing so. It also gave the United States the right to maintain a naval base on

In 1908, American occupation troops camped in front of the Presidential Palace in Havana, Cuba.

Guantanamo Bay. All of this made Cuba virtually a United States protectorate. The United States also endorsed Estrada Palma as Cuba's first president, which virtually assured his election.

In 1906, President Estrada Palma was forced to resign after a revolt occurred over the fixing of his reelection, and the United States again stepped in to prevent civil disturbances. American forces remained in Cuba for three years. In 1912, an insurrection by African Cubans, who demanded the same civil rights as other Cubans, again gave the United States a reason to intervene in Cuban affairs. Other minor interventions occurred in 1917 and 1920, both of them as the result of fraudulent elections. After the resignation of Estrada Palma as president, Cuba was governed by a series of weak and corrupt governments until General Gerardo Machado, who had fought in the War of Independence, was elected president in 1924.

At first, President Machado looked like the answer to Cuba's problems. His program included the rebuilding of a Cuba shattered by wars and corruption in government and the broadening of Cuba's economy. Unfortunately, a fall in the price of sugar and other economic problems led to strikes and demonstrations by workers and by students at Havana University. The government, of course, had to move to end the strikes and restore peace. This infuriated the strikers and students, and Machado took harsher steps to put them down. His government, and especially his police force, became more and more repressive.

In 1928, a Machado-controlled legislature voted to give him six more years in office, and he became, in reality, a dictator. The university students formed a secret organization in opposition to Machado and began resorting to assassinations and gun battles in the streets of Havana with Machado's brutal police. The United States could have intervened once again under the terms of the Platt Amendment. However, the situation was so heated that the government in Washington, D.C., hesitated to enter into it for fear of being drawn into a full-scale war with Cuba. The American ambassador to Cuba, Sumner Welles, tried to convince Machado to step down. This angered the students and workers even more because they wanted to deal with Machado themselves. Machado finally gave in and went into exile in 1933.

The Platt Amendment had long been criticized by Latin Americans as no more than a tool of "Yankee imperialism," and there was much opposition to it in the United States as well. With the downfall of Machado, Cubans experienced a wave of national pride and demanded that the Platt Amendment be done away with. The United States was in the midst of its worst depression ever, and it had enough troubles without opposing popular feelings at home and abroad. The Platt Amendment was withdrawn from the Cuban constitution in May 1934, under the terms of a treaty between the United States and Cuba and as part of the United States' wish to promote its new good-neighbor policy toward Latin America. The United States, however, was allowed to keep its naval base on Guantánamo Bay.

The government that followed Machado's could not control the situation. Revolutionary activity increased, with mobs attacking wealthy city dwellers and roving bands taking over sugar factories and looting the homes of landowners. In September 1933, a group of Cuban army noncommissioned officers revolted and forced the government to resign. Among the leaders of the coup was Sergeant Fulgencio Batista y Zaldívar. The army turned over the control of the government to a commission chosen by the university students. It was, in fact, the students who had taken the largest part in the revolution, and now they were firmly in control. Unfortunately, the new government was no more successful than the previous one; strikes, rioting, and gun battles became common throughout Cuba. Once again the army stepped in, this time led by Sergeant Batista, and took over the government. Batista was to rule the country, first from behind the scenes and then as an outright dictator, for the next eleven years, until 1944.

In 1933, the Cuban student organizations had become a real force in Cuban politics when they created a party which they claimed was based on the principles of José Martí. It had the grand title of the *Partido Revolucionario Cubano-Auténtico* (Authentic Cuban Revolutionary Party), but its followers were known as the *Auténticos*. This party remained the main opponent to Batista throughout his stay in power. Batista's main support came from the army, but he actually brought many reforms to Cuban government and genuine improvement to the economy and the conditions of laborers. He won a fair election in 1940, and during World War II he benefited Cuba by receiving aid from the United States, which was doing everything it could to strengthen the Western Hemisphere. However, Batista could not rid himself of the accusations of corruption and gangsterism, and the Auténticos never let up in their opposition to him. In 1944, he lost a fair election which he could have easily fixed in his favor. He retired to the United States, a multimillionaire.

The student movement, which reached its high point with the defeat of Batista, did not do much better in the national spotlight than had the corrupt parties it overthrew. It did, however, produce two remarkable men—Eduardo ("Eddie") R. Chibás and Fidel Castro.

Chibás was sickened by the wave of corruption and violence that erupted in Cuba after World War II. The price of sugar rose to spectacular heights, and the profits to be made from the booming economy created an atmosphere of greed and excess. Chibás broke away from the *Auténticos* and formed the *Ortodoxo* party, claiming that he was José Martí's true political heir. He ran for president in 1948 but lost to Carlos Prío Socarrás, who soon became involved in graft and corruption greater than that of any president before him. Socarrás also used Martí's words to discredit his opponent. He quoted Martí's poems in his speeches and claimed that Chibás could never understand the ideals of forgiveness and honesty that Martí represented. Both sides found something in Martí to use for their own purposes. Chibás continued to attack the government on weekly radio broadcasts, but without much success. He fell into despair and, after a final broadcast on August 5, 1951, shot himself.

Eddie Chibás's suicide plunged the nation into gloom. There seemed to be no way out of Cuba's problems, which all seemed to stem from her one-crop economy. Corruption, greed, and excess grew and the government made no attempt to halt any of it. Into this hopeless situation stepped, once again, Fulgencio Batista. Before the farce of the 1952 elections was about to take place, he returned from the United States and took over the government in a coup supported by army officers.

Batista again tried to better the life of the average Cuban. He restored law and order, even if it did consist of his brutal police force, and he tried to establish a program of public works. He could not overcome the weaknesses of Cuba's sugar economy, however, and as a result the standard of living of all Cubans was lowered. The condition of the small farmers and laborers who lived outside of the great cities was especially bad, and it was from them that Chibás's Ortodoxo Party got its chief support. The student movement was not dead; in fact, it was growing stronger because of the widening gulf between the rich and the poor of Cuba. The students had also never forgiven Batista for his overthrow of the constitution in 1940. They felt that tyranny was tyranny, no matter what it replaced, and tyranny must be removed.

Fidel Castro was a follower of Chibás and became a member of the more radical wing of the Ortodoxo Party while he was a student at Havana University. He had always been an admirer of José Martí, and throughout his career he insisted that he was following Martí's principles and ideals. On July 26, 1953, he attempted to overthrow Batista by attacking the army barracks at Santiago de Cuba. The attack was doomed from the start, and most of the young people who took part in it were either killed or captured. Castro escaped but was later captured and sentenced to prison. What saved him from execution was the fact that he

Cuban Premier Fidel Castro always claimed that he was a follower of Martí's principles. Like Martí, he experienced early imprisonment, exile, and guerrilla warfare in Oriente province.

had, overnight, become a national hero. Batista could not afford to go against such strong public opinion, so he spared the young revolutionary. At his trial, Castro gave his famous "History will absolve me" speech, in which he outlined his program for a Cuba that would be both free from the tyranny of a corrupt dictatorship and economically independent. Almost everything he proposed could be found in the writings and speeches of Martí. The majority of the Cuban people embraced Castro's ideas wholeheartedly, either outwardly or in secret.

When Castro was released from prison, in May 1955, he went to Mexico, where he founded the 26 July Movement, whose purpose was to invade Cuba and free it from the Batista dictatorship. He was joined in Mexico by other Cuban exiles. On December 2, 1956, Castro, together with eighty-two men, sailed for Cuba on the yacht *Granma* and landed in Oriente province. The revolution started there and ended a little over two years later, on January 1, 1959, when Batista fled Havana, and Fidel Castro and his forces entered the city in triumph.

It is interesting to note that during the early days of Castro's revolution, he was hiding in the Sierra Maestra mountains of Oriente province. His army was small and barely surviving, and the success of the rebels was in doubt. Castro was then visited by an American journalist, Herbert

Matthews of *The New York Times*, to whom Castro granted an exclusive interview. In 1957, Matthews began publishing in the *Times* a series of articles on Castro. It is said that these articles, more than anything else, turned world opinion in favor of Castro.

He became a hero to many in the United States, and public opinion moved Congress to cut off any aid to Batista. Does this sound familiar? Did Castro take a page from Martí's history, the one in which Martí granted an interview to George E. Bryson of *The New York Herald* while in the middle of his march from Las Playitas to Dos Ríos? In both cases, the intention was to sway public opinion in the United States.

Fidel Castro has always said that he is following in the footsteps of Martí, but many critics maintain that he has broken away from Martí's principles on several crucial points. The military organization that Castro formed has remained in power, and a dictatorship exists today that is at least as strong as Batista's. Castro made Cuba completely independent of the United States, but in so doing lost its number-one trading partner. He was forced to depend almost exclusively on the Soviet Union for support and aid. In other words, he traded the United States for the U.S.S.R. Freedom of expression was also stifled, and censorship and punishment for dissenting voices became commonplace. Many of Cuba's prominent writers, artists, and scientists left the country. This is certainly something that Martí would have considered a disaster.

CHAPTER TEN

THE APOSTLE

 After the Second War of Cuban Independence, which ended in 1898, the name of José Martí was remembered in Cuba by the veterans of the war and by his fellow poets and writers. Sometimes their praise of him was extravagant. Many began to refer to him as the "apostle," a name that was first given to him in 1889 by Gonzalo de Quesada, who later wrote of him: ". . . like Christ, he was the victim of mockery, he suffered injuries and ingratitude from the very ones whom he proposed to save."[1] He was remembered with great respect by the soldiers

and peasants who had known him during the war, but he was not too well-known among the middle class. His literary reputation was kept alive from abroad—from Latin America and Europe—and he had always been respected in New York.

After the downfall of the dictator Machado in 1933, however, Cubans began to look to their political heritage for inspiration in their efforts to govern themselves. Martí's name began to be mentioned more and more frequently in speeches, dedications, memorials, and all other events in which Cuba displayed its pride in its past history. Politicians began to invoke his name when praising their party or program, whether they were liberal, conservative, or reactionary. If a political party was out of power, it would quote Martí to the effect that all government was corrupt and controlled by wealthy landowners or American business executives. If a party was *in* power, it would urge the people to follow Martí's example of trust, forgiveness, and unity for the good of all. In death, Martí became a man for all seasons and every political outlook.

The rebirth of the Cuban people's pride in their heritage after the removal of the Platt Amendment from their constitution and their increased awareness of themselves as a free people brought about a renewal of interest in

Martí. The new nation needed heroes, and Martí fit the bill perfectly. During the late 1930s he was well on his way to becoming a national legend. His likeness began to appear on postage stamps, coins, and medals. Statues of him were placed at prominent intersections and in parks in all the major cities; there were contests among architects to design fitting memorials to him.

Biographies of Martí began to appear, and his huge literary output began to be edited and arranged in a final edition. Words were formed from his name. *Martiano* referred to anyone or anything that reflected the ideals of Martí; *Martiniano* meant something that applied to Martí; *Martista* designated a person who acted politically as Martí would have; *Martiolatría* was the worship of Martí; and, of course, *Martianismo* covered just about everything to do with Martí. One of his most famous poems, one which is known to just about every Cuban, is titled *Rosa Blanca* (White Rose). When a Cuban wants to compliment someone, he or she will say "Rosa Blanca."[2] There was even a patriotic group called *La Orden de la Rosa Blanca* (The Order of the White Rose) whose large membership was devoted to spreading the gospel as written by José Martí. At one time this group published a monthly magazine called *La Rosa Blanca* and had its own radio program that featured readings from the master's works.

All this began to verge on idolatry and, at times, appeared a little silly. The hundredth anniversary of Martí's birth was celebrated in 1953, and the committee chosen to oversee the festivities decided to make a motion picture of the apostle's life. Since film facilities in Cuba were limited, they chose a Mexican company to make the picture. Unfortunately, the film company picked a Mexican actor to portray Martí, and a lot of the film was shot in Mexico. An uproar erupted in the Cuban press. Newspaper columnists and editorial writers howled that their own beloved Martí ended up speaking with a Mexican accent and looking like an "Aztec."[3] The controversy that raged over the film *La Rosa Blanca* lasted for months, and many people still feel that the fuss it caused was much more entertaining than the film itself.

Then, in 1956, Warner Brothers studio in Hollywood quite innocently included the character of Martí in one of its movies. The movie, called *Santiago*, starred Alan Ladd and Lloyd Nolan. It was about the Spanish-American War, which Cubans now call the Hispanic-Cuban-American War, and had a scene in which Martí is interviewed by American soldiers of fortune who have volunteered to fight for Cuba. Unfortunately, the year is 1898, three years after Martí's death, and the interview takes place in a gorgeous mansion in Haiti, with Martí surrounded by luxury. Another uproar followed this film's showing. Critics took it as an insult to the Cuban people and a deliberate attempt to belittle their national hero. One critic called it "a case of open aggression."[4] Radicals urged all Cubans to rise up against this national insult by the United States. The producers in Hollywood must have been puzzled by the reaction in Cuba. After all, they often rewrote history to fit the romantic plots of their movies, and nobody ever seemed to mind.

Martí is connected with Hollywood in another way. In 1880, when Martí first arrived in New York, he stayed in a boardinghouse owned and run by a woman named Carmen Miyares de Mantilla. Some time after he moved in, Carmen gave birth to a daughter, María. It is widely believed that Martí was María's father. Normally, this would be just another rumor whispered about famous people after they die, but when María grew up she had a child who became a well-known movie star, César Romero. Romero always claimed to be Martí's grandson and took pride in the fact.[5] When one sees the tall, powerfully built, handsome, and confident César Romero on film,

Many believe that José Martí was the father of María Mantilla.

however, it is hard to imagine that he is the grandson of the frail, shy, unassuming poet and scholar who wrote, *"Cultivo una rosa blanca"* ("I grow a white rose").[6]

The fame of José Martí has grown under the Castro regime as never before. Havana's central square, library, and airport are named after him. His works are widely read and have become part of the nation's school curriculum. His poetry is read aloud, memorized by schoolchildren, and set to music. The folk song "Guantanamera," which uses Martí's words, is known throughout the world and is used as an anthem by any group that has any cause whatsoever to promote.

As might be expected, Cuban exiles and other anti-Castro groups also use Martí's words to condemn the oppressive regime in Cuba. They regularly broadcast into Cuba news and opinion from the outside world over their own radio station in Florida. The name of their station? Radio Martí.

José Martí continues to be a living presence for all Cubans, regardless of their politics. He stood for some basic principles that hold for everyone: individual freedom, the rights of people to determine their own destiny, and a tolerance for all races and beliefs. Along with this went a love of literature, art, music, philosophy, and learning that is almost unique in a national leader and hero.

César Romero had an active career in Hollywood from the 1930s through the 1970s.

The man himself would probably be embarrassed by all this fame and adulation. He tried to avoid the spotlight, even though his cause required him to become a public figure. He cared more for his country than for himself. He fought for it throughout his life and sacrificed himself for it willingly and with forgiveness:

> *Cultivo una rosa blanca*
> *En julio como en enero,*
> *Para el amigo sincero*
> *Que me da su mano franca.*
>
> *Y para el cruel que me arranca*
> *El corazón con que vivo,*
> *Cardo ni oruga cultivo:*
> *Cultivo la rosa blanca.*[7]
>
> (I grow a white rose
> In July as in January,
> For the sincere friend
> Who gives me his open hand.
>
> And for the cruel one who tears out
> The heart that gives me life,
> I cultivate neither thistle nor worm,
> I grow a white rose.)

CHRONOLOGY

1853—José Julián Martí y Pérez is born on January 28 in Havana, Cuba.

1865—Martí is enrolled in the Municipal School for Boys in Havana.

1868—The first war of independence, later called the Ten Years War, begins in Cuba.

1869—Martí is accused of treason and imprisoned in Havana City jail.

1870—Martí is sentenced to six years of hard labor. The sentence is reduced, and he is transferred to the Isle of Pines.

1871— Martí is deported to Spain.

1873— King Amadeus of Spain abdicates, and the first Spanish republic is formed.

1874—The first Spanish republic falls. Martí completes his university education and leaves for Paris.

1875— Martí moves to Mexico.

1876—Porfirio Díaz comes to power in Mexico. Martí leaves Mexico for Cuba.

1877— Martí arrives in Havana but leaves shortly for Mexico and then Guatemala. Martí is appointed professor of literature and history of philosophy at the Central School of Guatemala, and marries Carmen Zayas Bazán in Mexico.

1878—The first war of independence ends. Martí sails for Havana in September. His son, José, is born in November.

1879—*La Guerra Chiquita* (The Little War) breaks out and is crushed. Martí is again deported to Spain. He then leaves Spain and travels to New York.

1880—Martí reaches New York and begins writing for New York newspapers. The Little War ends.

1881— Martí is appointed professor in Venezuela. He returns to New York in July.

1882—Martí publishes his first book of poems, *Ismaelillo* (Little Ishmael), and completes *Versos libres* (Free Verses).

1884—Martí resigns from revolutionary movement led by Máximo Gómez, and is appointed consul for Uruguay in New York.

1890—Martí helps establish *La Liga* (The League) in New York to promote education among African Cubans.

1891— Martí visits Tampa, Florida, and writes the *Tampa Resolutions* and *Bases of the Cuban Revolutionary Party.*

1892—Martí becomes delegate of Cuban Revolutionary Party and travels to Dominican Republic to meet with Máximo Gómez.

1893—Martí meets with Antonio Maceo in Costa Rica and invites him to join the revolutionary movement.

1894—Martí organizes Fernandina plan for invasion of Cuba.

1895—Fernandina plan fails. Martí travels to Santo Domingo to join Máximo Gómez. He lands in Cuba on April ll, and is killed in battle at Dos Ríos on May 19.

1898—United States enters war against Spain, which lasts three months. United States military occupation begins.

1902—Cuban government signs Platt Amendment. United States occupation ends.

1952—Fulgencio Batista overthrows Cuban government and returns to power as dictator on March 10.

1959—Fidel Castro forces Batista to flee Cuba and takes over as head of government in February.

Chapter Notes

CHAPTER 1

1. José Martí, "Diary: From Cabo Haitano to Dos Ríos," in *Our America: Writings on Latin America and the Struggle for Cuban Independence*, ed. Philip S. Foner and trans. Elinor Randall (New York: Monthly Review Press, 1977), p. 419.

2. José Martí, "To Manuel Mercado," *Our America*, p. 439.

3. Ibid.

4. José Martí, "To Federico Henriquez y Caravajal," *Our America,* pp. 402–403.

CHAPTER 2

1. José Martí, *Versos sencillos*, I.

CHAPTER 3

1. R. B. Gray, *José Martí, Cuban Patriot* (Gainesville, Fla.: University of Florida Press, 1962), p. 2.

2. José Martí, *Versos sencillos*, XXX.

3. Gray, p. 4.

CHAPTER 4

1. José Martí, *Inside the Monster: Writings on the United States and American Imperialism*, ed. Phillip S. Foner and trans. Elinor Randall (New York: Monthly Review Press, 1975), p. 22.

2. José Martí, *Versos sencillos*, III.

3. José Martí, *Versos sencillos*, IX.

CHAPTER 5

1. José Martí, "Letter to Manuel Mercado," in R. B. Gray, *José Martí, Cuban Patriot* (Gainesville, Fla.: University of Florida Press, 1962), p. 11.

2. José Martí, *Inside the Monster: Writings on the United States and American Imperialism*, ed. Phillip S. Foner and trans. Elinor Randall (New York: Monthly Review Press, 1975), pp. 26–27.

3. Ibid. p. 27.

4. Ibid.

5. Ibid.

CHAPTER 6

1. Introduction to *José Martí: Major Poems*, ed. Philip S. Foner and trans. Elinor Randall (New York: Holmes & Meier, 1982), p. 8.

2. José Martí, "Hijo," *Ismaelillo*.

3. R. B. Gray, *José Martí, Cuban Patriot* (Gainesville, Fla.: University of Florida Press, 1962), p. 17.

4. Ibid. p. 18.

5. Ibid. p. 19.

6. Todd M. Appel, *José Martí* (New York: Chelsea House Publishers, 1992), p. 52.

7. José Martí, *Inside the Monster: Writings on the United States and American Imperialism*, ed. Phillip S. Foner and trans. Elinor Randall (New York: Monthly Review Press, 1975), p. 331.

8. Ibid. p. 32.

9. "Gabriel García Márquez Meets Ernest Hemingway," *The New York Times Book Review* (July 26, 1981).

10. José Martí, *On Art and Literature: Critical Writings by José Martí*, ed. Phillip S. Foner and trans. Elinor Randall (New York: Monthly Review Press, 1982), p. 18.

11. Ibid. p. 20.

12. Ibid. p. 27.

13. José Martí, "Letter to Manuel Mercado," in *Our America: Writings on Latin America and the Struggle for Cuban Independence*, ed. Philip S. Foner and trans. Elinor Randall (New York: Monthly Review Press, 1977), p. 440.

CHAPTER 7

1. José Martí, *Our America: Writings on Latin America and the Struggle for Cuban Independence*, ed. Philip S. Foner and trans. Elinor Randall (New York: Monthly Review Press, 1977), p. 16.

2. Todd M. Appel, *José Martí* (New York: Chelsea House Publishers, 1992), p. 59.

3. Ibid.

4. R. B. Gray, *José Martí, Cuban Patriot* (Gainesville, Fla.: University of Florida Press, 1962), p. 21.

5. Appel, p. 61.

6. Gray, p. 24.

7. Ibid.

CHAPTER 8

1. Todd M. Appel, *José Martí* (New York: Chelsea House Publishers, 1992), p. 91.

2. R. B. Gray, *José Martí, Cuban Patriot* (Gainesville, Fla.: University of Florida Press, 1962), pp. 29–30.

3. Introduction to *José Martí: Major Poems*, ed. Philip S. Foner and trans. Elinor Randall (New York: Holmes & Meier, 1982), pp. 13–14.

4. José Martí, "Diary: From Cabo Haitano to Dos Ríos," *Our America: Writings on Latin America and the Struggle for Cuban Independence,* ed. Philip S. Foner and trans. Elinor Randall (New York: Monthly Review Press, 1977), p. 406.

5. Gray, pp. 30–31.

6. Ibid.

7. Appel, p. 19.

CHAPTER 10

1. R. B. Gray, *José Martí, Cuban Patriot* (Gainesville, Fla.: University of Florida Press, 1962), p. 133.

2. Ibid. p. 134.

3. Ibid. pp. 137–138.

4. Ibid. p. 139.

5. Ibid. pp. 14, 264.

6. José Martí, *Versos sencillos*, XXXIX.

7. Ibid.

GLOSSARY

abdicate—To give up a throne or other position of power.

Cortes—The parliament, or legislature, of Spain.

coup—An overthrow of a government by force.

Criollo—A person of Spainish descent born in Latin America.

depression—A period of decline in a country's economy, causing business failures and unemployment.

émigré—A person forced to leave his country for political reasons.

exile—A forced separation from one's country. A person who is forced to leave his own country and live in another.

filibuster—An irregular military operation, usually undertaken without approval of government.

grito—A shout or cry. A name for a political declaration or a call to action.

guerrilla—A member of a band of soldiers who operate outside of a military organization.

junta—A small group of people who take over a country after a revolution or overthrow of a government.

liberal—A person who favors progress or reform in politics.

lyceum—A lecture hall.

manifesto—A declaration of purposes or intentions.

peninsular—A person who is born in Spain but lives in Latin America.

underground—An organization or army that operates in secret.

voluntario—A member of a group attached to or working for the Spanish army or militia.

FURTHER READING

Appel, Todd M. *José Martí*. New York: Chelsea House Publishers, 1992.

Gray, Richard Butler. *José Martí, Cuban Patriot*. Gainesville, Fla.: University of Florida Press, 1962.

Kirk, John M. *José Martí: Mentor of the Cuban Nation*. Tampa, Fla.: University of South Florida Book, University of Florida Press, 1983.

Martí, José. *The America of José Martí, Selected Writings*. trans. Juan de Onís. New York: Noonday Press, 1953.

———. *Inside the Monster: Writings on the United States and American Imperialism*. ed. Phillip S. Foner and trans. Elinor Randall. New York: Monthly Review Press, 1973.

———. *José Martí: Major Poems, A Bilingual Edition*, ed. Phillip S. Foner and trans. Elinor Randall. New York: Holmes & Meier, 1982.

———. *On Art and Literature: Critical Writings by José Martí*. ed. Phillip S. Foner and trans. Elinor Randall. New York: Monthly Review Press, 1982.

————. *Our America: Writings on Latin America and the Struggle for Cuban Independence.* ed. Phillip S. Foner and trans. Elinor Randall. New York: Monthly Review Press, 1977.

Williamson, Edwin. *The Penguin History of Latin America.* New York: Allen Lane, The Penguin Press, 1992.

INDEX